Production Notes

CASTING

Two Narrators are suggested, preferably with different voice timbres for contrast. They may be male and female or both women. Six Readers are recommended in addition to the Narrators. No great acting ability is necessary, but the readers should be able to speak clearly and with a sense of the drama in their words. They should know the lines well enough so that they can frequently look at the person to whom they are speaking.

The parts may be divided as follows. The readers, except Jesus, may also join with the Crowd and Soldiers.

Reader 1 — Jesus
Reader 2 — Prophet, Disciple 1, Elder, Priest 3
Reader 3 — Pilate, Priest 1, Disciple 2, Elder
Reader 4 — Jeremiah, Priest 2, Elder
Reader 5 — Judas, Elder, Priest 4
Reader 6 — Peter, Centurion, Angel
Reader 7 — Pilate's Wife, Two Girls (Unless assigned to the choir)

The voices of the Crowd and Soldiers are the choir members. Each person should select one phrase in each series. This is repeated until a climax is reached and the director signals a stop. The following single lines should be assigned to appropriate and willing choristers: Slave, Witnesses, Man, Woman, Girls, Pilate's Wife.

STAGING

This drama is intended to be a reading rather than an acted play. It is a complete worship service which should last about an hour, though we have found that the congregation becomes so wrapped in the story that they do not object if the hour runs late.

The Narrators may be placed one on either side of the chancel; if possible elevated above the other readers. The readers should be in a semi-circle facing the congregation but placed

5

so that they can look toward the person to whom they are speaking. Our choir loft was behind the readers so they became part of the scenes and action. In one church, the choir and organ were in the back balcony. It was still effective.

This drama can be presented with three rehearsals. One for the choir, one for the readers and one for both combined. Of course the choir had previously learned the music.

MUSIC

Music often speaks more directly to our hearts than words alone. The hymns are placed in the narrative to permit the congregation to ponder the events as they occur in the story and to give them a sense of participation in the drama. The anthems (or solos) were chosen to reflect on the scene or to express our reactions to the Passion as it unfolds.

I have listed the hymns which we found most effective. However, you may choose alternate hymns if the suggested ones are unfamiliar. This is not the time to teach new hymns. The number of verses sung depends on your time limits and how they fit into the drama.

These are some of the various anthems which we have used. I am not including the publishers because new anthems go out of print so quickly and the classic anthems are available from many sources. However, the titles will give you text ideas which you can adapt to your own music library and to the abilities of your singers. These may also be replaced by hymns or solos.

Anthem 1 — "I Believe This Is Jesus" (Spiritual)
"Daughter Of Zion, Shout For Joy" (Handel)

Anthem 2 — "Psalm 51, Have Mercy On Me" (Gelineau)
"When Jesus Wept" (Billings)

Anthem 3 — "Have You Seen My Jesus" (Wagner)
"Behold The Lamb Of God" (Handel)

Anthem 4 — "With His Stripes We Are Healed" (Handel)
"Jesus In Thy Dying Woes" (Sateren)
"All Ye That Pass By" (Pergolesi)

Anthem 5 — "What Wondrous Love Is This" (Spiritual) ·
"O Come And Mourn With Me" (Hopson)

Anthem 6 — "God So Loved The World" (Stainer)

Order Of Service

Organ Prelude

Call To Worship

Hymn: "Lift Up Your Heads"

And Him Crucified — Dramatic Reading

I. Jesus Enters Jerusalem (Matthew 21:1-11)
Choral Response

II. The Passover Supper (Matthew 26:1-35)
Hymn: "The Lord's My Shepherd" (vv. 1, 2, 3)

III. The Garden Of Gethsemane (Matthew 26:36-56)
Choral Response

Unison Prayer of Confession
Most merciful God,
    we confess it is for us that Jesus weeps,
    for we have sinned against you in thought,
      word, and deed;
    we have not loved you with our whole heart;
    we have not loved our neighbors as ourselves.
We pray you in your great mercy,
    forgive what we have been, amend what we are,
    direct what we shall be;
    that we may delight in your will and walk in
      your ways
    through Jesus Christ our Lord, who has taught
      us to pray:
    "Our Father ..."

IV. Peter's Denial (Matthew 26:57-75)
Choral Response

Reception Of The Offering
Organ Offertory

V. Jesus Before Pilate (Matthew 27:1-26)
Choral Response

VI. The Crucifixion (Matthew 27:27-38)
Hymn: "O Sacred Head Now Wounded"

VII. The Mockery (Matthew 27:39-44)
Choral Response

VIII. The Finish (Matthew 27:45-56)
Choral Response

IX. The Entombment (Matthew 27:57-66)

Prayer of Intercession
Unto you, Holy Father, we come in praise
through Jesus Christ: who for our sins was lifted
up upon the cross, that he might draw all men
to himself; who by his suffering and death became the way of eternal salvation to all who
trust him.
For all your children near and far we humbly pray.
And especially for those whose needs are known
to us:
(Time for silent intercessions)
For the assurance of your care, for the comfort of
your grace, we give you thanks. Amen.

X. The First Day (Matthew 28:1-10, 20b)
Choral Response

Hymn: "When I Survey The Wondrous Cross"

Benediction

Organ Postlude

anò him Crucifieò

Organ Prelude

Call To Worship

Hymn: "Lift Up Your Heads" or "Rise Up, O Men Of God"

I. Jesus Enters Jerusalem

Narrator 1: The Passion of our Lord according to Saint Matthew. When they had come near Jerusalem and had reached Bethphage *(Beth'-fah-gay),* at the Mount of Olives, Jesus sent two disciples, saying to them:

Jesus: Go into the village ahead of you. Immediately you will find a donkey tied, and a colt with her. Untie them and bring them to me. If anyone says anything to you, just say this, "The Lord needs them." He will send them immediately.

Narrator 1: This took place to fulfill what had been spoken through the prophet.

Prophet: Tell the daughter of Zion, look, your king is coming to you, humble, and mounted on a colt, the foal of a donkey.

Narrator 1: The disciples went and did as Jesus had directed them; they brought the donkey and the colt, and put their cloaks on them, and he sat on them. A very large crowd spread their cloaks on the road and others cut branches from the trees and spread them on the road.

(Crowd noises begin)

The crowds that went ahead of him and that followed were shouting.

9

(Each crowd person selects one phrase. He stands as he speaks. Crowd voices overlap and repeat. Growing louder until the director stops them.)

Crowd 1: Hosanna! Hosanna!
Crowd 2: Hosanna to the Son of David!
Crowd 3: Blessed is the one who comes!
Crowd 4: Blessed is the name of the Lord!
Crowd 5: Name of the Lord! Hosanna!
Crowd 6: Hosanna in the highest!

Narrator 1: When he entered Jerusalem, the whole city was in turmoil, asking,

(Crowd whispers and crescendos, overlapping lines and repeating, then fading away)

Crowd 1: Who is this?
Crowd 2: Who? Who? Who is it?
Crowd 3: This is the prophet!
Crowd 4: Prophet Jesus!
Crowd 5: Jesus from Nazareth!
Crowd 6: Jesus of Galilee!

Anthem 1: *(See Production Notes)*

II. The Passover Supper
Narrator 1: Jesus said to his disciples,

Jesus: You know that after two days the Passover is coming, and the Son of Man will be handed over to be crucified.

Narrator 1: Then the chief priests and the elders of the people gathered in the palace of the high priest, who was called Caiaphas *(Ki-a-fas)*, and they conspired to arrest Jesus by stealth and kill him.

Priest 1: Not during the festival!

Priest 2: There may be a riot among the people!

Narrator 2: Now while Jesus was at Bethany in the house of Simon, the leper, a woman came to him with an alabaster jar of very costly ointment. She poured it on his head as he sat at the table. But when the disciples saw it, they were angry.

Peter: Why this waste?

Judas: This could have been sold for a large sum!

Disciple 1: And given to the poor.

Narrator 2: But Jesus, aware of this, said to them,

Jesus: Why do you trouble the woman? She has performed a good service for me. By pouring this ointment on my body she has prepared me for burial. Truly I tell you, wherever this good news is proclaimed in the whole world, what she has done will be told in remembrance of her.

Narrator 2: Then one of the 12, who was called Judas Iscariot, went to the chief priests and said,

Judas: What will you give me if I ... if I ... betray him to you?

Narrator 2: They paid him 30 pieces of silver. And from that moment he began to look for an opportunity to betray him.

Narrator 1: On the first day of Unleavened Bread the disciples came to Jesus.

Peter: Where do you want us to make the preparations for you to eat the Passover?

Jesus: Go into the city to a certain man. Say to him, "The Teacher says, 'My time is near: I will keep the Passover at your house with my disciples.' "

Narrator 1: So the disciples did as Jesus directed them, and they prepared the Passover meal. When it was evening, he took his place with the 12; while they were eating, he said,

Jesus: Truly I tell you, one of you will betray me.

Narrator 1: They became greatly distressed and began to say to him one after another,

Disciple 1: Is it ... I, Lord?

Peter: Surely, not I?

Disciple 3: I, Lord?

Jesus: The one who has dipped his hand into the bowl with me ... will betray me. The Son of Man goes as it is written of him, but woe to that one by whom the Son of Man is betrayed! It would have been better for that one not to have been born.

Narrator 1: Judas who betrayed him, said,

Judas: Surely not ... I, ... Rabbi?

Jesus: *(Looks at Judas and pauses)* You have said so.

Narrator 2: While they were eating, Jesus took a loaf of bread, after blessing it he broke it, and gave it to the disciples.

Jesus: Take, eat; this is my body.

Narrator 2: Then he took a cup, and after giving thanks he gave it to them.

Jesus: You have said so ... But I tell you, from now on you will see the Son of Man seated at the right hand of Power ... and coming on the clouds of heaven!

Narrator 1: Then the high priest tore his clothes.

Priest 2: He has BLASPHEMED! Why do we STILL need witnesses? You have now heard his blasphemy. What is your verdict?

Elders: *(Two or three of the readers shout at random)* Death! Death! He deserves death!

Narrator 1: Then they spat in his face and struck him. Some slapped him.

Elders: *(At random, high pitched, with laughter)* Prophesy to us, you Messiah! Who is it that struck you?

Narrator 2: Now Peter was sitting outside in the courtyard, when a servant girl came by.

Girl 1: Weren't you with Jesus? The Galilean?

Peter: I don't know what you're talking about.

Narrator 2: When he went out to the porch, another servant girl saw him. She said to the bystanders,

Girl 2: This man was with Jesus of Nazareth.

Peter: I DO NOT know the man!

Narrator 2: After a little while some bystanders came up to Peter.

Man: Certainly you're one of them. Your accent betrays you.

Narrator 2: Then Peter began to curse, and he swore an oath,

Peter: I DO NOT KNOW THE MAN!

Narrator 2: At that moment the cock crowed. Then Peter remembered what Jesus had said:

Jesus: Before the cock crows, you will deny me three times.

Narrator 2: He went out ... and wept bitterly.

Anthem or Hymn: "Out Of The Depths I Cry To Thee" *(vv. 1 and 2)*

Reception Of The Offering With Organ Offertory

V. Jesus Before Pilate

Narrator 1: When morning came, all the chief priests and elders of the people conferred together against Jesus in order to bring about his death. They bound him, led him away, and handed him over to Pilate, the governor. When Judas, his betrayer, saw that Jesus was condemned, he repented and brought back the 30 pieces of silver to the chief priests and the elders.

Judas: I have sinned by betraying innocent blood.

Priest 3: What is that to us? See to it yourself!

Narrator 1: Throwing down the pieces of silver in the temple, he departed ... He went and hanged himself ... But the chief priests, taking the pieces of silver, said,

Priest 2: It is not lawful to put them into the treasury, since they are blood money.

Narrator 1: After conferring together, they used them to buy the potter's field as a place to bury foreigners. For this reason that field has been called the Field of Blood to this day. Then was fulfilled what had been spoken through the prophet Jeremiah.

Jeremiah: They took the 30 pieces of silver, the price of the one on whom some of the people of Israel had set a price, and they gave them for the potter's field, as the Lord commanded me.

Narrator 1: Now Jesus stood before the governor

Pilate: Are you the King of the Jews?

Jesus: You say so.

Narrator 1: But when he was accused by the chief priests and elders, he did not answer. Then Pilate said,

Pilate: Do you not hear how many accusations they make against you?

Narrator 1: But he gave no answer, not even to a single charge, so that the governor was greatly amazed. Now at the festival the governor was accustomed to release a prisoner for the crowd, anyone they wanted. At that time they had a notorious prisoner, called Jesus Barabbas. So after they had gathered, Pilate said to them,

Pilate: Whom do you want me to release for you, Jesus Barabbas or Jesus who is called the Messiah?

Narrator 1: He realized that it was out of jealousy that they had handed Jesus over. While he was sitting on the judgment seat, his wife sent word to him.

Pilate's Wife: Have nothing to do with that innocent man, for today I have suffered a great deal because of a dream about him.

Narrator 1: Now the chief priests and elders persuaded the crowds to ask for Barabbas and to have Jesus killed. *(Crowd murmurs begin)* The governor again said to them,

Pilate: Which of the two do you want me to release for you?

Crowd: *(Murmurs rise to a roar. One voice shouts, "Barabbas," rest join in at random.)*

Pilate: Then what should I do with Jesus who is called the Messiah?

Crowd: *(Each person selects a numbered phrase and repeats at random)* (1) Let him be crucified! (2) Death! (3) Crucify him! (4) Let him die! (5) Away with him!

Pilate: Why, what evil has he done?

Crowd: *(At random louder)* (1) Let him be crucified! (2) Away with him! (3) Death! (4) Crucify him! (5) Let him die!

Narrator 1: So when Pilate saw that he could do nothing, but rather that a riot was beginning, he took water and washed his hands before the crowd.

Pilate: I am innocent of this man's blood. See to it yourselves.

Crowd: *(At random as before)* (1) His blood be on us! (2) On us and our children!

Narrator 1: So he released Barabbas for them; and after flogging Jesus, he handed him over to be crucified.

Anthem 3

VI. The Crucifixion

Narrator 2: Then the soldiers of the governor took Jesus into the governor's headquarters. They gathered the whole cohort around him. They stripped him and put a scarlet robe on him. After twisting some thorns into a crown, they put it on his head. They put a reed in his right hand and knelt before him and mocked him.

Soldiers: *(Repeat at random with laughter and hoots)* Hail! King! Hail King of the Jews!

Narrator 2: They spat on him, and took the reed and struck him on the head. After mocking him, they stripped him of the robe and put his own clothes on him. Then they led him away to crucify him. *(Long pause)*

Narrator 1: As they went out, they came upon a man from Cyrene named Simon. They compelled this man to carry the cross. When they came to a place called Golgotha (which means Place of a Skull), they offered him wine to drink, mixed with gall. But when he tasted it, he would not drink it. *(Pause)*

Narrator 2: When they had crucified him, they divided his clothes among themselves by casting lots. Then they sat down there and kept watch over him. Over his head they put the charge against him, which read, "This is Jesus, the King of the Jews."

Narrator 1: Then two bandits were crucified with him, one on his right and one on his left.

Hymn: "O Sacred Head Now Wounded" or "Ah Holy Jesus"

VII. The Mockery

Narrator 1: Those who passed by derided him, shaking their heads, *(Crowd noises begin and continue through priests' lines)*

Man: You who would destroy the temple and build it in three days, save yourself!

Woman: If you're the Son of God, come down from the cross!

Narrator 2: In the same way the chief priests, along with the scribes and elders, were mocking him.

Priest 1: He saved others; He cannot save himself.

Priest 2: HE is the king of Israel?

Priest 3: Let him come down from the cross.

Priest 2: THEN we will believe in him.

Priest 1: He trusts in God; Let God deliver him.

Priest 3: If he wants to! *(Crowd noise ends)*

Priest 2: He said, "I am God's Son!"

Narrator 1: The bandits who were crucified with him also taunted him in the same way.

Anthem 4

VIII. The Finish

Narrator 2: From noon on, darkness came over the land until three in the afternoon. About three o'clock Jesus cried with a loud voice,

Jesus: ELI! Eli, lema sabachthani? *(Ay-lee! ay-lee, lay-ma say-bahk-thah-nye)* My God, my God, why have you forsaken me?

Woman: He's calling for Elijah.

Narrator 1: At once one of them ran and got a sponge, filled it with sour wine, put it on a stick, and gave it to him to drink.

Man: Wait, let's see if Elijah will come to save him!

Narrator 2: Then Jesus cried again with a loud voice and breathed his last.

(Silence)

Anthem 5

IX. The Entombment

Narrator 1: At that moment the curtain of the temple was torn in two, from top to bottom. The earth shook. The rocks were split. The tombs were opened, and many bodies of the saints who had fallen asleep were raised. After his resurrection they came out of the tombs and entered the holy city and appeared to many.

Narrator 2: Now when the centurion and those with him, who were keeping watch over Jesus, saw the earthquake and what took place, they were terrified.

Centurion: Truly, this man was the Son of God!

Narrator 1: Many women were also there, looking on from a distance. They had followed Jesus from Galilee and had provided for him. Among them were Mary Magdalene, and Mary the mother of James and Joseph, and the mother of the sons of Zebedee.

Narrator 2: When it was evening, there came a rich man from Arimathea, *(Air-e-ma-thee-ah)* named Joseph. He was also a disciple of Jesus. He went to Pilate and asked for the body, wrapped it in a clean linen cloth, and laid it in his own new tomb, which he had hewn in the rock. He then rolled a great stone to the door of the tomb and went away. Mary Magdalene and the other Mary were there, sitting opposite the tomb.

Narrator 1: The next day, after the day of preparation, the chief priests and the Pharisees gathered before Pilate.

Priest 4: Sir, we remember what that imposter said while he was still alive, "After three days I will rise again." Therefore command the tomb to be made secure until the third day. Otherwise his disciples may go and steal him away, and then tell people, "He has been raised from the dead." The last deception would be worse than the first.

Pilate: You have a guard of soldiers! Go, make it as secure as you can.

Narrator 2: So they went with the guard and made the tomb secure by sealing the stone and setting a guard.

Unison Prayer Of Intercession (Narrator 1)
Unto you, Holy Father,
>we come in praise through Jesus Christ;
>who for our sins was lifted up upon the cross,
>that he might draw all men to himself;
>who by his suffering and death became the way
>of eternal salvation to all who trust him.

For all your children near and far we humbly pray,
>and especially for those whose needs are known to us:
>>*(Time for silent intercessions)*

For the assurance of your care,
>for the comfort of your grace,
>we give you thanks. Amen.

X. The First Day
Narrator 1: After the sabbath, as the first day of the week was dawning, Mary Magdalene and the other Mary went to see the tomb. Suddenly there was a great earthquake; for an angel of the Lord, descending from heaven, came and rolled back the stone and sat on it. His appearance was like lightning, and his clothing white as snow. For fear of him the guards shook and became like dead men. But the angel said to the women,

Angel: Do not be afraid! I know that you are looking for Jesus who was crucified. He is not here; for he has been raised, as he said. Come, see the place where he lay. Then go quickly and tell his disciples, "He has been raised from the dead, and indeed he is going ahead of you to Galilee. There you will see him." This is my message for you.

and
him
Crucified

a Service for passion Sunday
With Readers' theater
Based on Matthew

Bettie Scott

CSS publishing Company, Inc.
Lima, Ohio

AND HIM CRUCIFIED

Acknowledgements

I would like to thank my husband Robert F. Scott for his encouragement, advice, and for the use of his computer. He also composed the two unison prayers which are included in the drama. My thanks go also to all of the people who have participated in the productions of this dramatic reading.

ISBN 1-55673-701-7   PRINTED IN U.S.A.

"For I have decided to know nothing among you except Jesus Christ, and him crucified."
— 1 Corinthians 2:2

TO HIS GLORY

Jesus: Drink from it, all of you; for this is my blood of the covenant, which is poured out for many for the forgiveness of sins. I tell you, I will never again drink of this fruit of the vine until that day when I drink it new with you in my Father's kingdom.

(Communion may be served at this point.)

Hymn: "The Lord's My Shepherd" vv. 1, 2, 3

III. The Garden Of Gethsemane

Narrator 1: When they had sung the hymn, they went out to the Mount of Olives. Then Jesus said to them,

Jesus: You will all become deserters because of me this night; for it is written, "I will strike the shepherd, and the sheep of the flock will be scattered." But after I am raised up, I will go ahead of you to Galilee.

Narrator 1: Peter said to him,

Peter: Even though I must die with you, I will not deny you.

Jesus: Truly, I tell you, this very night, before the cock crows, you will deny me three times.

Peter: Even though I must die with you, I will not deny you.

Narrator 1: So said all the disciples. Then Jesus went with them to a place called Gethsemane. He said to his disciples,

Jesus: Sit here while I go over there and pray.

Narrator 2: He took with him Peter and the two sons of Zebedee, and began to be grieved and agitated.

Jesus: I am deeply grieved, even to death; remain here, and stay awake with me.

Narrator 2: Going a little farther, he threw himself on the ground and prayed.

Jesus: My Father . . . if it is possible . . . let this cup pass from me; . . . yet not what I want but what you want.

Narrator 2: Then he came to the disciples and found them sleeping. He said to Peter,

Jesus: So . . ., could you not stay awake with me one hour? Stay awake and pray that you may not come into the time of trial. The spirit indeed is willing, but the flesh is weak.

Narrator 2: He went away for the second time and prayed,

Jesus: My Father, if this cannot pass . . . unless I drink it, your will be done.

Narrator 2: Again he came and found them sleeping, for their eyes were very heavy. So leaving them again, he went away and prayed for the third time, saying the same words. Then he came to the disciples.

Jesus: Are you still sleeping and taking your rest? See, the hour is at hand. The Son of Man is betrayed into the hands of sinners. Get up! Let us be going. See! My betrayer is at hand.

Narrator 2: While he was still speaking, Judas, one of the 12, arrived. With him was a large crowd with swords and clubs, *(Crowd murmurs begin)* from the chief priests and the elders of the people. Now the betrayer had given them a sign.

Judas: The one I will kiss is the man. Arrest him!

Narrator 2: At once he came up to Jesus,

Judas: Greetings, Rabbi.

Narrator 2: And he kissed him. *(Crowd murmurs stop)*

Jesus: Friend, do what you are here to do.

Narrator 2: Then they came and laid hands on Jesus and arrested him. Suddenly, one of those with Jesus put his hand on his sword, drew it, and struck the slave of the high priest, cutting off his ear.

Slave: *(Screams)* Ay-e-e-e-e!!

Jesus: *(To Peter)* Put your sword back into its place. All who take the sword will perish by the sword. Do you think that I cannot appeal to my Father? He will at once send me more than 12 legions of angels. But how then would the scriptures be fulfilled, which say it must happen in this way?

(To Soldier) Have you come out with swords and clubs to arrest me ... as though I were a bandit? Day after day I sat in the temple teaching. You did not arrest me. But all this has taken place, so that the scriptures may be fulfilled.

Narrator 2: Then all the disciples deserted him and fled.

Anthem 2

Unison Prayer Of Confession (Narrator 2)
Most merciful God,
    we confess it is for you that Jesus weeps,
    for we have sinned against you in thought, word and deed;
    we have not loved you with our whole heart;
    we have not loved our neighbors as ourselves.

15

We pray you in your great mercy,
>   forgive what we have been, amend what we are,
>   direct what we shall be;
>   that we may delight in your will and walk in your ways
>   through Jesus Christ our Lord, who has taught us to pray:

"Our Father ..."

IV. Peter's Denial

Narrator 2: Those who had arrested Jesus took him to Caiaphas the high priest, in whose house the scribes and elders had gathered. Peter was following him at a distance, as far as the courtyard of the high priest. Going inside, he sat with the guards in order to see how this would end.

Narrator 1: Now the chief priest and the whole council were looking for false testimony against Jesus so that they might put him to death. They found none, though many false witnesses came forward. At last two came forward and said,

Witness 1: *(Stands)* This fellow said, "I'm able to destroy the temple of God."

Witness 2: *(Stands)* And build it in three days!

Narrator 1: The high priest stood up and said to him,

Priest 1: Have you no answer? ... What is it that they testify against you?

Narrator 1: But Jesus was silent.

Priest 1: I put you under oath before the living God ... Tell us if you are the Messiah ... the Son of God.

Narrator 2: They left the tomb quickly with fear and great joy, and ran to tell his disciples. Suddenly Jesus met them. They came to him, took hold of his feet and worshiped him.

Jesus: Do not be afraid; go and tell my brothers to go to Galilee; there they will see me. Remember, I am with you always, to the end of the age.

Anthem 6 *(Optional)*

Hymn: "When I Survey The Wondrous Cross" or "Beneath The Cross Of Jesus"

Benediction

Organ Postlude